Jazz In Focus

Jazz Improv

Edwin McLean and Kevin Olson

An Introduction to Jazz

To the Student

Jazz has been around for over 100 years. Back around 1900, Scott Joplin and others made ragtime wildly popular. By 1910, the blues had become an established style. Early jazz combined these two styles, along with other influences: European, Latin, Caribbean.

So what is jazz? Duke Ellington's song said famously, "It don't mean a thing if it ain't got that swing." But not all jazz is swung. However, it is usually improvised (made up on the spot). A jazz performance typically starts with a tune, such as a popular song; then the players take solos; finally, the tune is repeated to end the piece. Harmonically, jazz is usually based on seventh chords, which we'll study in this book.

People who play and teach jazz professionally often think of the "bebop" style of the 1940s–1950s as the gold standard for being a real player. This style was developed by Charlie Parker (sax), Dizzy Gillespie (trumpet), Theolonius Monk (piano), and others. The harmony is based on seventh chords and even more complicated chords and scales, and songs are usually swung hard and fast. If you worked through *Blues Improv*, you already know how to swing eighth notes.

Jazz Improv is meant as an introduction to a very big subject. We hope it opens the door for further study. The best way to learn jazz, though, is to listen to it! Check out the Discography on page 44. Many of the pieces from these classic albums are available on YouTube.

Above all, have fun!

Edwin McLean

Kevin Olson

CONTENTS

4

To the Teacher

Jazz Improv is the third book in the Improv series, designed to introduce students of all ages to jazz improvisation. *Pop Improv* introduces improvisation to elementary students who may have never improvised before. *Blues Improv* is a level higher and teaches students how to play swing style, learn the basic blues scale and chord progression, as well as idiomatic patterns and riffs. Ideally, *Blues Improv* should be studied before beginning *Jazz Improv*, since blues is an important aspect of jazz. The book also discusses the dominant 7th chord and the mixolydian mode, concepts which carry over into *Jazz Improv.* For students who have not gone through *Blues Improv,* Unit 1 reviews the most important concepts.

Jazz Improv is divided into eight units. Each unit has four modules:
1. A concept page which covers the topic of the unit.

2. A short original piece that illustrates the unit concept. This piece may be played by the teacher to demonstrate the feel of the improv.

3. A "riff improv" which consists of several easily memorized riffs that the student can combine in any order while the teacher plays the written accompaniment (or the recording can be used instead).

4. An improvisation chart which allows the student to make up his/her own improv patterns.

Students may need to play the final improv (number 4 above) with only the right hand. If even this is too hard, students can memorize some of the riffs already learned and play them in addition to (or instead of) original licks. For really shy students, a "copy cat" approach often works: While the recording is playing, the teacher can play a few notes (even just two or three) and have the student echo them an octave higher. Building confidence is crucial: If a student plays "wrong" notes, or the rhythm isn't all that jazzy—well, let it slide. Learning to improvise is a gradual process. Some students may not ever get the hang of making up their own licks. But even if they go through all but the last module in the unit, they will have learned a lot about how to feel and play jazz.

How to use the Downloadable Recordings (Tracks)

We recommend that the student download the recordings to an iPod or smart phone, so they can cue up tracks as needed, and practice at home with headphones or speakers. During the lesson using the recording allows the teacher to observe the student without having to play the teacher parts. It's also easier to "copy cat" with the student, as discussed previously.

Each track is numbered in the book. Set the volume low enough so that the students can easily hear themselves above the accompaniment.

Original pieces are played as piano solos. It is not necessary for the student to learn the pieces as repertoire; they may be too hard for some students to read and learn quickly. Their main purpose is to illustrate the unit concept and prepare the student for the next module.

The longest tracks are the final free improvs at the end of each unit. It's not necessary to play the entire track; it can be stopped at any time.

Discography

Every jazz buff has his/her own list of favorite albums. Yours may not be on the list. We have tried to focus on albums which are not only important, but also feature the piano. Piano students will relate more to piano, bass, and drums than groups that feature a sax or trumpet player. Of course, some albums are so important that they can't be ignored, such as *Kind of Blue*.

Listening to albums or songs from a discography presumes a lot from any student. Our experience is that using such lists requires a jump start. So spend a few minutes of each improv lesson listening one or two songs from an album. Some jazz songs run long, so feel free to turn them off after a few minutes. Discussing what you've heard with your student can be fun and educational for both teacher and student.

UNIT 1

The Blues (review)

Learning to play the blues is a basic skill for learning jazz. Most jazz players can play the blues, but not all blues players can play jazz! A good example of a jazz player who relies heavily on blues is Oscar Peterson; go to YouTube and listen to him play *C Jam Blues*, as a starting point.

In *Blues Improv* we learned how to swing eighth notes. Not all jazz is played with a swing, but a lot of it is.

We also learned the basic blues scale, played with the R.H.:

The basic blues scale

(or G♭)

Check out the
Power Blues Scale
at the bottom of
page 43.

The dominant 7th chord
For the L.H., we use dominant 7th chords.

To review, **a dominant 7th chord is a major triad with a minor 7th above the root**:

G major triad   minor 7th   G7

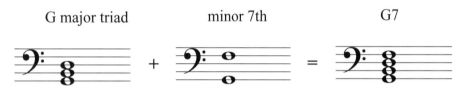

The blues chord progression
Blues has a 12-bar repeated pattern of I, IV, and V chords, shown below in C major.

C	C	C	C
F	F	C	C
G	F	C	C

Below is the pattern, presented as "shells." (Only the bottom and top notes are used.)

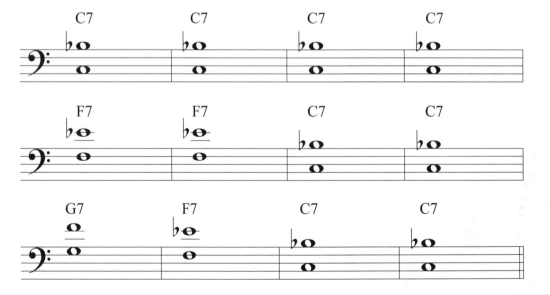

The Down-Home Blues

Brightly, with a swing (♩ = ca. 144) (♫ = ♩³♪)

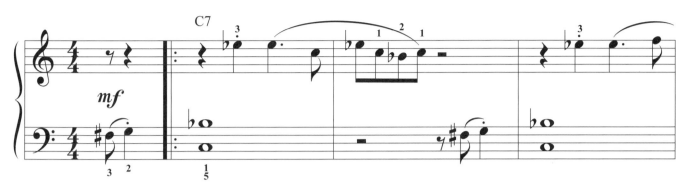

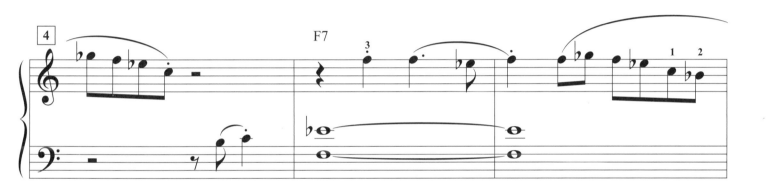

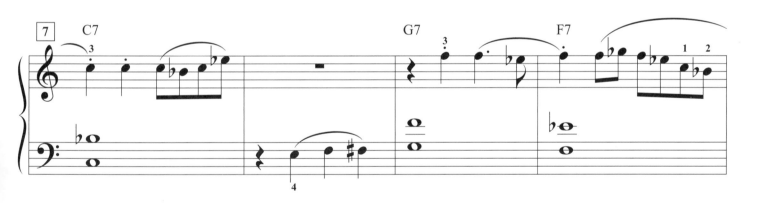

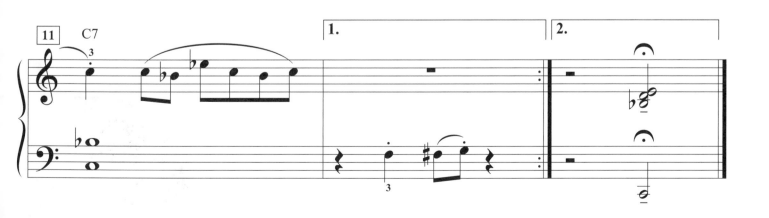

Riffin' the Blues

A *riff* is a short melodic idea that you can use when improvising.

First learn the R.H. riffs below. Be sure to play them with a swing.

Your teacher will then play the 12-bar blues. Answer each riff you hear with one of the riffs below, in any order.

(You can also practice *Riffin' the Blues* at home with the downloadable recording.)

Swing the ♩♩'s

Teacher Part: (Student plays 1 octave higher)

L.H. 8va lower throughout

Down-Home Blues Improv

Now that you've played a blues piece and some riffs, try making up your own improv following the chart below.

Play with a relaxed swing. You can improvise as a solo, with your teacher, or with the recording. If you have trouble playing hands together, practice R.H. alone with the recording.

Play R.H. 8va higher, with swing

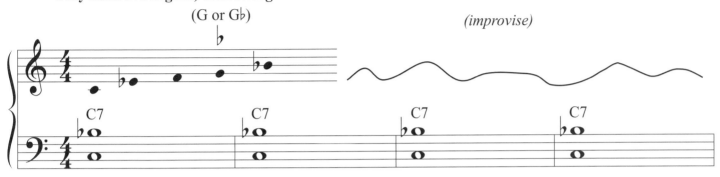

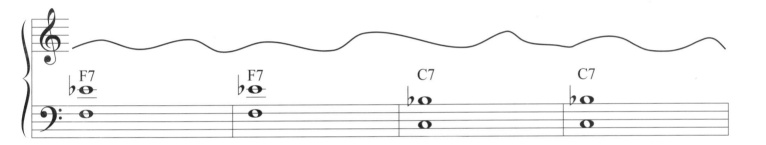

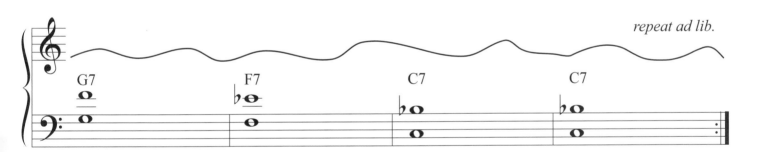

Teacher Part: (Student plays as written)

FJH2248

UNIT 2
The Major 7th Chord

Jazz harmony is based on "seventh chords"—chords that have a 7th above the root,
in addition to the basic triads. Here are seventh chords built from the notes of a C major scale:

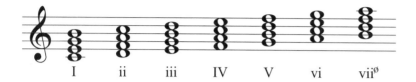

You already know that the V chord is a dominant 7th chord (discussed in the previous unit).
The I chord and the IV chord are also major 7th chords—the other ones will be discussed in a later unit.

Major 7th chords are built by adding the interval of a **major 7th** above the root. This interval is only 1/2 step less
than an octave.

So what does this chord sound like? Obviously it sounds major, because it contains a major triad.
And the major 7th above the root gives it a bright quality.

In jazz the major 7th chord can be named a couple of different ways.

The letter name is followed by **maj7**: **Cmaj7** **Dmaj7** **E♭maj7**

Another common notation is to use a triangle instead of "maj." CΔ7 DΔ7 E♭Δ7

You will see both of these in jazz lead sheets.

Write and play
In the boxes below write a major 7th chord above the given note.
First build a major triad, then add a major 7th above it.
Make sure to use a major 7th above the root—it will be the note that is 1/2 step less than an octave.
After writing them, play them and listen to the quality of the sound.

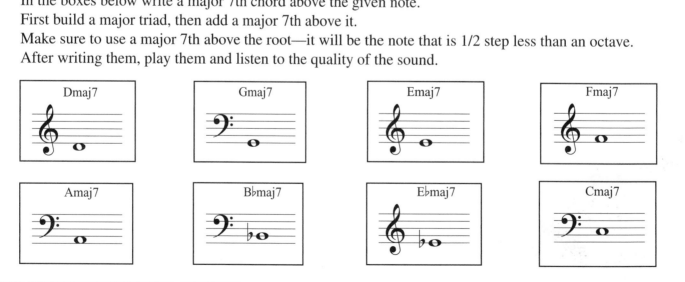

A Sunny Day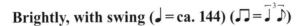

This piece uses the Cmaj7 and Fmaj7 chords.
To make the piece easier to play, the 3rd of each chord has been omitted.

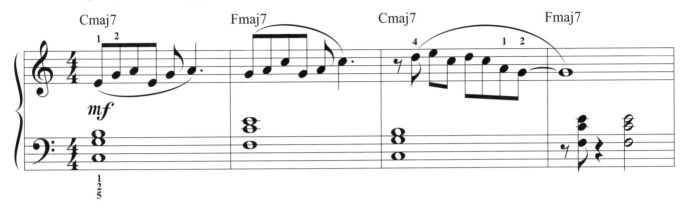

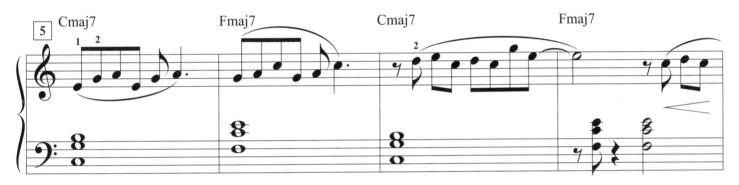

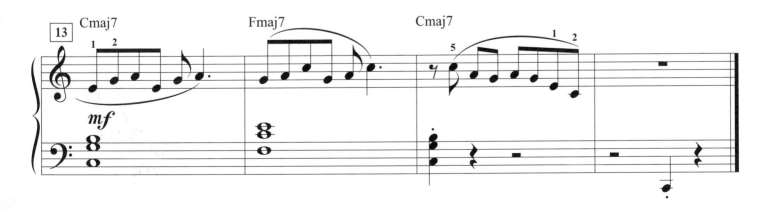

Sunny Riffs ⑤

Play the riffs in any order. Play each riff *twice* before going to a new riff. The riffs will work with both the Cmaj7 and the Fmaj7 chords. With your R.H., play a lazy swing while your teacher plays the accompaniment, or you can play along with the recording.

Teacher Part: (Student plays 1 octave higher)

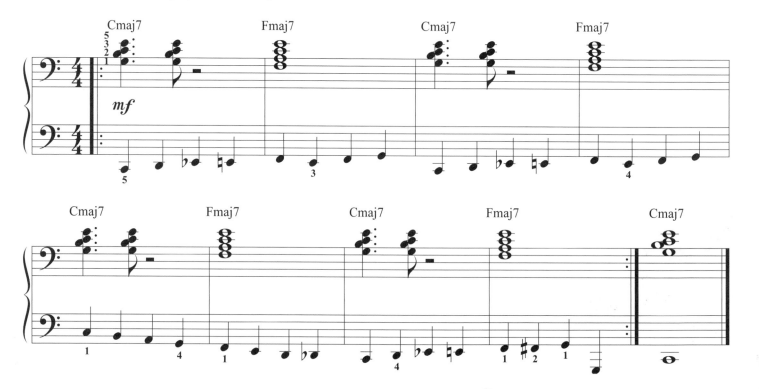

Sunny Day Improv ⑥

Play with a relaxed swing. You can improvise as a solo, with your teacher, or along with the recording for the feeling of being in a jazz group.

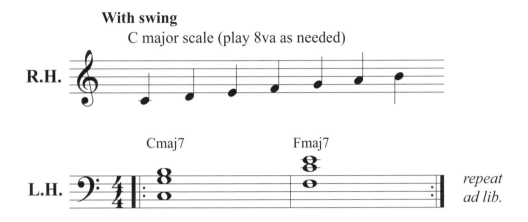

Teacher Part: (Student plays as written)

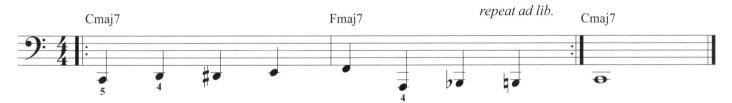

UNIT 3

The Minor 7th Chord

Look back on page 10 for the 7th chords built on ii, iii, and vi.
These are **minor 7th** chords.

Minor 7th chords are built with a minor triad, and a **minor 7th** above the root.
A minor 7th is a whole step less than an octave.

What does a minor 7th chord sound like? Well, it sounds minor, and instead of sounding bright like a major 7th chord, it has a darker, "cooler" quality.

In jazz the minor 7th chord can also be named a couple of different ways.

The letter name is followed by **m7**:   **Cm7**   **Dm7**   **E♭m7**

Another common notation is to use a dash instead of "**m**."   **C-7**   **D-7**   **E♭-7**

You will see both of these in jazz lead sheets, although the dash isn't quite as common as the triangle used for major 7th chords.

Write and play

In the boxes below write a minor 7th chord above the given note.
First build a minor triad, then add a minor 7th above it.
Make sure to use a minor 7th above the root—it will be the note that is a whole step less than an octave.
After writing them, play them and listen to the quality of the sound. Notice they sound darker and cooler.

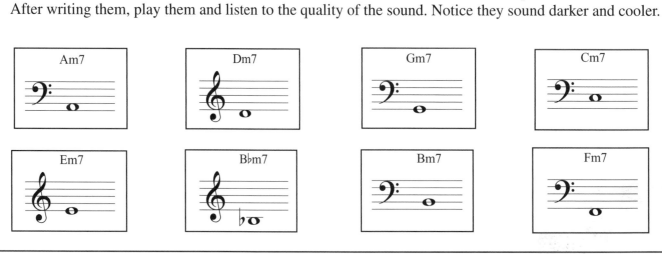

Evening Breeze ⑦

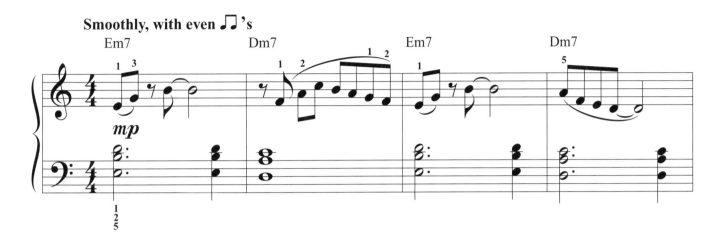

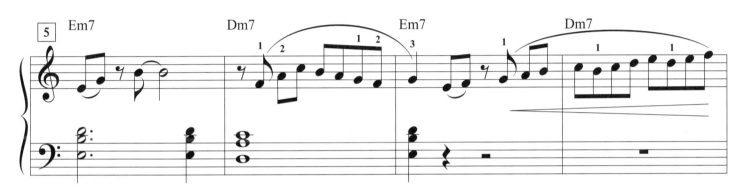

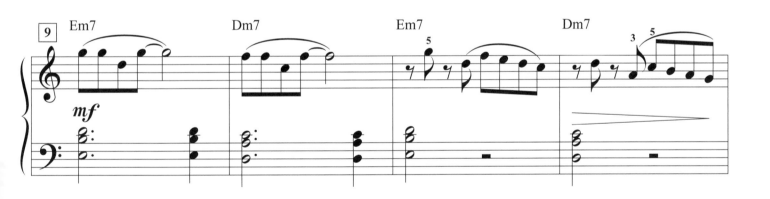

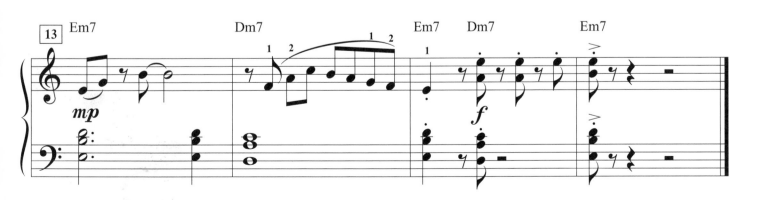

Breezy Riffs ⑧

With your R.H., play the riffs in any order. Play each riff *twice*.

Your teacher will accompany you, or you can play along with the recording.

Listen to the groove as you play.

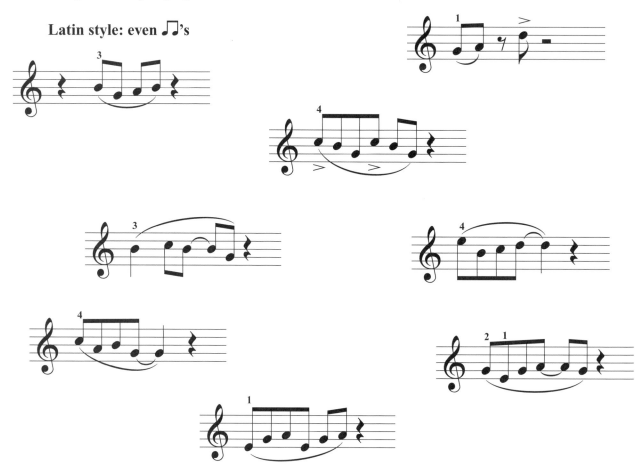

Latin style: even ♫'s

Teacher Part: (Student plays as written)

Breezy Improv (9)

No swing on this improv—it's Latin style.

With your R.H. play any white-key melodies in the range as shown.
L.H. plays whole notes, unless you feel confident enough to add a little rhythm (♩. ♪♩) .

Play as a solo, with your teacher, or along with the recording.

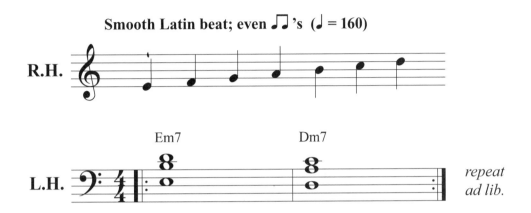

Teacher Part: (Student plays as written)

Play 8va lower throughout

UNIT 4
The Major ii-V-1 Chord Progression

The ii-V-I chord progression is the most important progression in jazz.
In the key of C major, it is built from the notes of the scale:

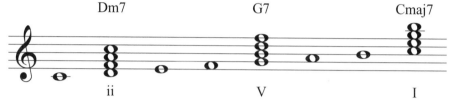

Notice that the ii chord is a minor 7th chord, the V chord is a dominant 7th chord, and the I chord is a major 7th chord. We've already discussed these chords in previous units, so review them if you need to.

> In this unit, we'll "voice" the L.H. chords so they are easier to play. Voicing means rearranging the notes of the chords, which requires omitting some of the notes:

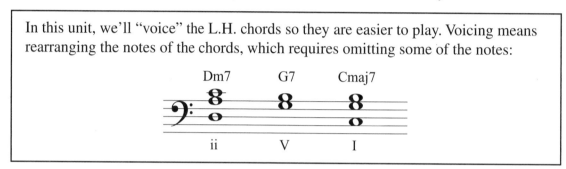

Jazz songs use ii-V-I progressions that may not be in the key of the piece.
For example, in Miles Davis classic 1953 song *Tune Up*, the chord progression looks like this:

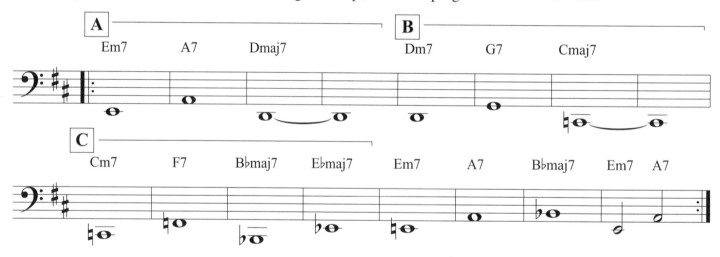

A   *Tune Up* is in the key of D major, so the first ii-V-I is in the key of D.
(The bass movement is E-A-D, which is ii-V-I in D major.)

B   The next ii-V-I suggests the key of C major.
(The bass notes are D-G-C in C major.)

C   The next ii-V-I suggests the key of B♭ major.
(The bass notes are C-F-B♭ in B♭ major.)

You can see that **any** three chords can make up a ii-V-I progression, as long as they fit with each other.
It's the relationship of the three chords to each other that's important.
Listen to the song on YouTube, and you will hear the same 16-measures repeated over and over, while Miles improvises his solo.
Most jazz songs use combinations of ii-V-I chord progressions.

Route 251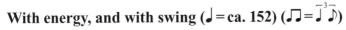

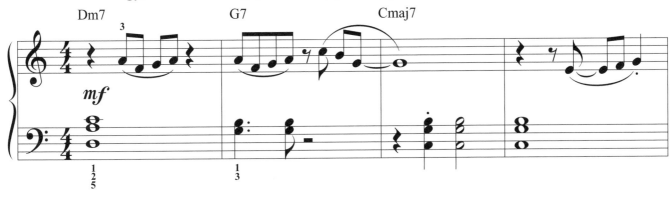

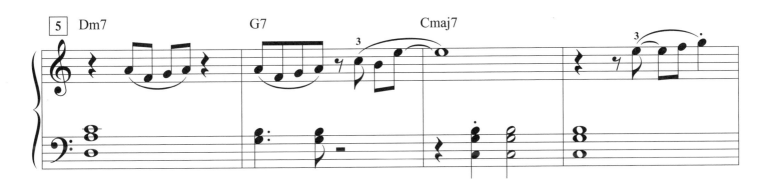

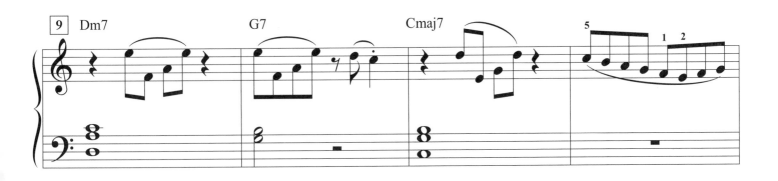

Major ii-V-I Riffs

Play the 6 riffs in any order. You can repeat them if you like.

With your R.H., play a cool bebop-style swing while your teacher plays the accompaniment, or you can play along with the recording.

Teacher: For practice, clap rhythms with student (observing the accents).

Teacher Part: (Student plays as written, or 8va)

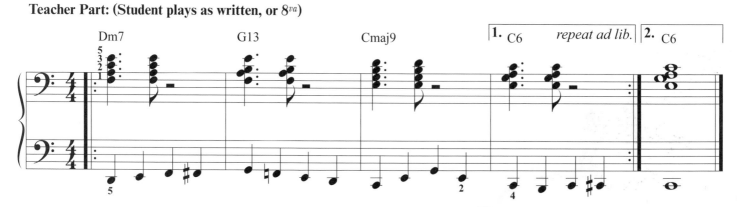

FJH2248

Major ii-V-I Improv ⑫

Make up your own riffs, using the notes of the C major scale.
You can also mix your own riffs with the ones from the previous page.
There are no wrong notes, but chord tones (notes that are part of the chord) always work!

Play as a solo, with your teacher, or along with the recording.

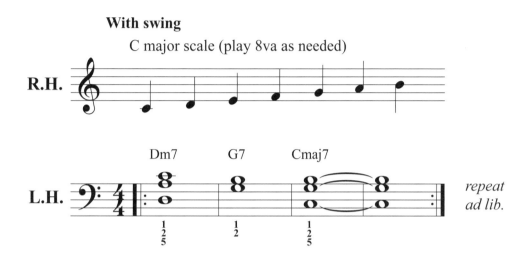

With swing

C major scale (play 8va as needed)

Teacher Part: (Student plays as written)

UNIT 5
The Minor ii-V-i Chord Progression

The minor ii-V-i chord progression is similar to the major ii-V-I.
In the key of A minor, it is built from the notes of the scale:

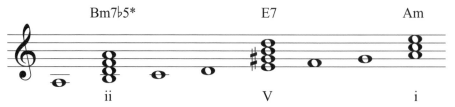

* also notated as B⌀7

The half-diminished 7th chord

The ii chord is a minor 7th chord with a flat 5. This means that
the 5th of the chord is not a perfect 5th—it's a "diminished" 5th:

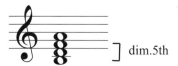

The half-diminished 7th chord has a unique quality—it sounds
different from the three other 7th chords we've already learned
(major 7, minor 7th, and dominant 7th).

A good example of a ii-V-i progression in a minor key is the classic jazz song, *Softly, As in a Morning Sunrise*.
Listen to the Sonny Clark Trio's 1957 recording on YouTube.
You'll hear the same ii-V-i progression repeated in the key of C minor:

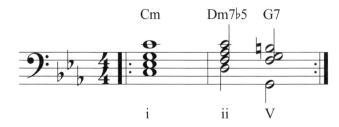

In this unit, we'll learn how to play the ii-V-i in A minor, using these voicings.

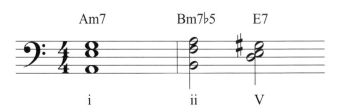

In A Minor Mood ⓭

Medium Latin style; even ♫'s (♩=132)

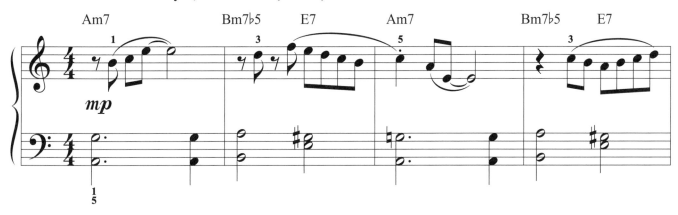

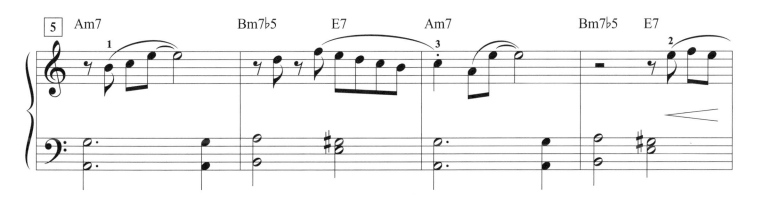

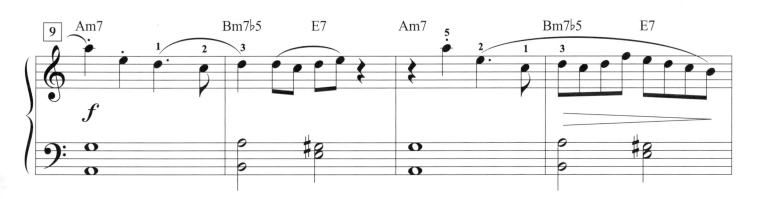

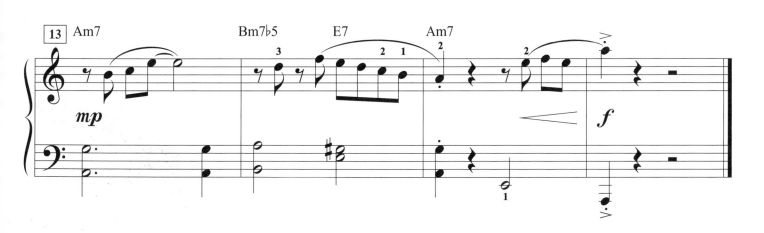

Minor ii-V-i Riffs ⑭

Play the riffs in any order.
You can also repeat the same one before going to a new riff.

With your R.H., play the riffs—Latin style (no swing)—while your teacher plays the accompaniment, or you play along with the recording.

Latin style, even ♫'s

Teacher Part: (Student plays as written or 8va)

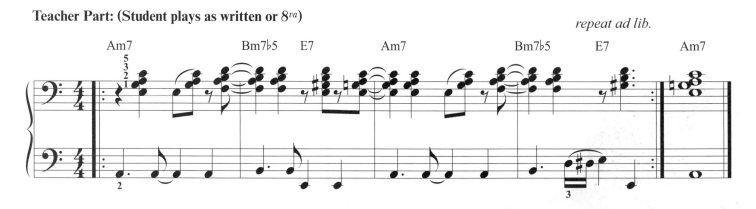

repeat ad lib.

Am7   Bm7♭5   E7   Am7   Bm7♭5   E7   Am7

Minor ii-V-i Improv ⑮

Make up your own riffs, using the notes of the A minor scale.
You can also mix your own riffs with the ones from the previous page.
There are no wrong notes, but chord tones always work.

Play as a solo, with your teacher, or along with the recording.

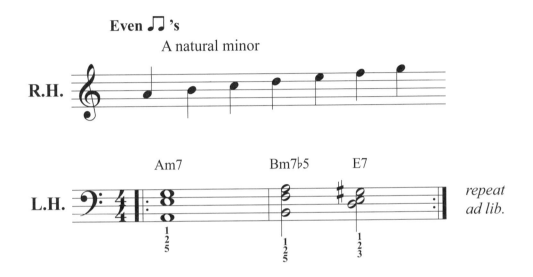

Teacher Part: (Student plays as written)

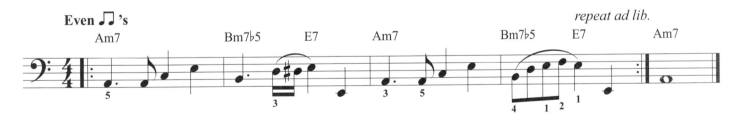

UNIT 6

Rhythm Riffs

This unit shows you how to take the same 3 or 4 notes and change the rhythm—which is a great way to make your jazz improvisations more interesting and exciting.

The riffs in this unit are based on the mixolydian scale (discussed in *Blues Improv*).
To review, a mixolydian scale is a major scale with a lowered 7th degree:

Jazz players often ascend to the 7th note of the mixolydian scale, using short rifts.
This riff uses notes 3 5 6 and 7 of the C mixolydian scale.

You can take this same riff and repeat it across more than one measure, like this:

Here's the same riff, on F mixolydian:

Listen to how Theolonius Monk uses 4-note rhythm riffs in his classic song *Epistrophy* (see Discography on page 44).
In the next piece *Rhythm-atic*, see how these riffs are varied by rearranging the notes and rhythm.

Rhythm-atic 16

Energetic, with swing ($\quarternote$ = ca. 144) ($\eighth\eighth$ = $\overset{3}{\triplet{\quarternote\eighth}}$)

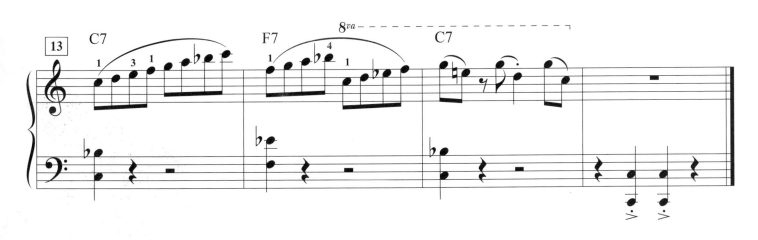

FJH2248

Rhythm-atic Riffs 🄹

Play the riffs in any order.

Each riff has two parts—a 2-measure C7 riff, and the same riff transposed up a 4th for F7. With your R.H., play a cool bebop-style swing while your teacher plays the accompaniment, or you play along with the recording.

Teacher: For practice, clap rhythms with student (observing the accents).

Teacher Part: (Student plays as written)

Rhythm-atic Improv ⑱

Make up your own riffs, using the given notes.
Remember that going up to the 7th creates an authentic jazz sound.
Also notice that the L.H. holds each chord for two measures.

Play as a solo, with your teacher, or along with the recording.

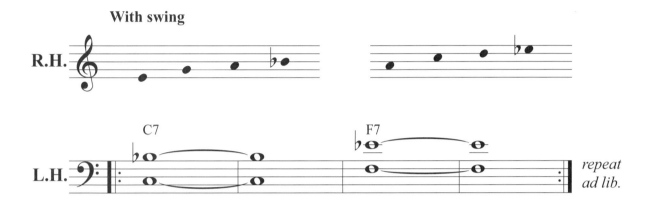

Teacher Part: (Student plays as written)

UNIT 7
Ascending Approach Tones

Every note of a chord can have its own "leading tone."
Jazz players call these "approach tones"—they ascend (go up) to the chord tone by a half step:

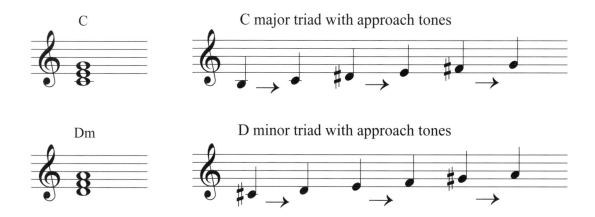

Approach tones can be used to create cool sounding riffs and melodies based on chords.
Play each riff below, then circle the approach tones.

riff on a C major triad   riff on a C major triad   riff on a D minor triad

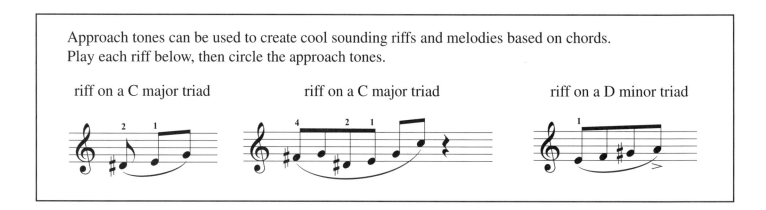

Here's a melody built on chord tones and approach tones.
First play it, then circle all of the approach tones.

Here's a piece that uses only two chords: Cmaj7 and Dm7.
Circle the approach tones in the two chords below:

Cmaj7

Dm7

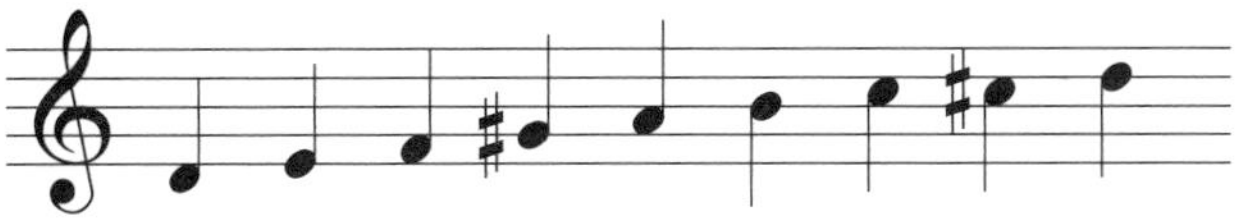

Notice how approach tones are used as you play *Ascension Jam*.

Ascension Jam ⑲

Medium swing (♩ = ca. 136) (♫ = ♩³♪)

Approach Etude ㉟

Teacher Part

With a medium swing

Approach Etude ㉑

Student Solo

When played as a solo, you can play with R.H. only or with both hands.
When played with the teacher accompaniment, use only your R.H..

Ascension Riffs ㉒

Play each riff twice, first from the Cmaj7 column on the left, then from the Dm7 column on the right.

With your R.H., play a cool bebop-style swing while your teacher plays the accompaniment, or you can play along with the recording.

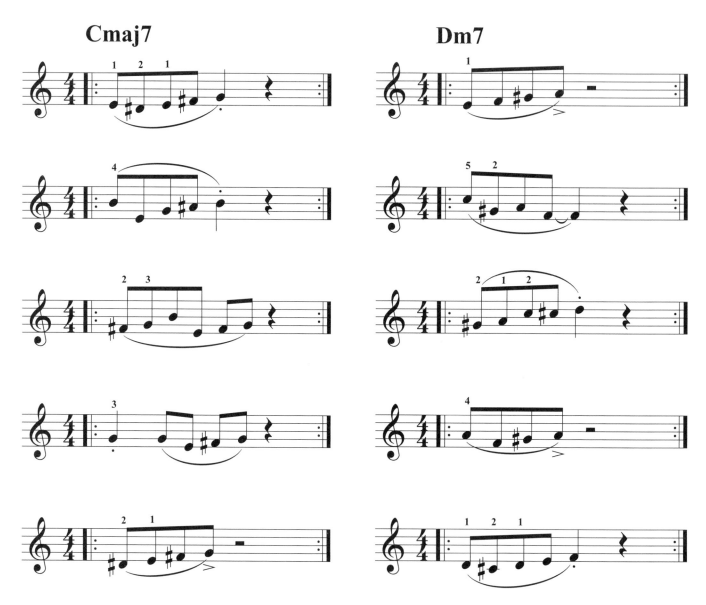

Extra credit: Circle the ascending approach tones in the above riffs.

Teacher Part: (Student plays as written with recording, or 8va with teacher)

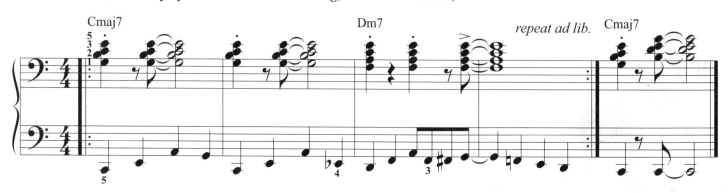

Ascension Improv ㉓

Warm-up improv
Practice this Power Scale to help you get started.

Now make up R.H. riffs against the two L.H. chords.
You can also use riffs from the previous page.

Notice that the L.H. changes chords every two measures.
You can play solo, with your teacher, or with the track.

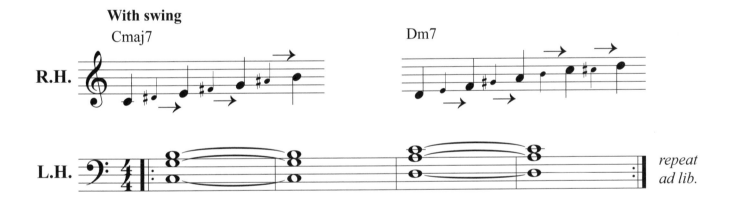

Teacher Part: (Student plays as written)

FJH2248

UNIT 8
Descending Approach Tones

Every note of a chord can also be approached from above.
The descending note goes down to the chord note.

We learned that ascending approach tones go up a half step.
Descending approach tones use the notes of the scale you're playing.

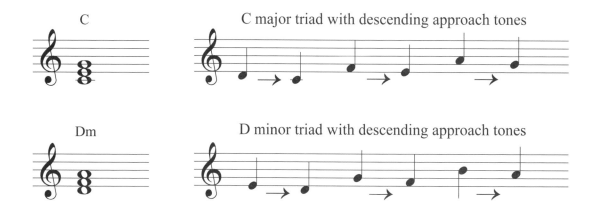

Using both ascending and descending approach tones can create some great sounding licks.
Play each riff below, then circle the approach tones, ascending and descending.

Here's a melody built on chord tones and approach tones.
First play it, then circle all of the approach tones, both ascending and descending. Hint: There are eight. *

*Answer: D♯ A♯ D | A G♯ | E G♯ | B |

Descension Jam ㉔

This piece uses the same two chords as in *Ascension Jam*: Cmaj7 and Dm7.
Notice how the melody includes both ascending and descending approach tones.

Descension Riffs ㉕

This improv uses the same chords as *Ascension Riffs*, except that descending approach tones are also used.

Play each riff *twice*.
First play any Cmaj7 riff from the left column,
then play any Dm7 riff from the right column.

Teacher Part: (Student plays as written with recording, or 8*va* with teacher)

Descension Improv

Improvise using chord tones.
The big notes are chord tones; the little notes are approach tones.
Each note of a chord can be approached by going up to it, or down to it—
like this example:

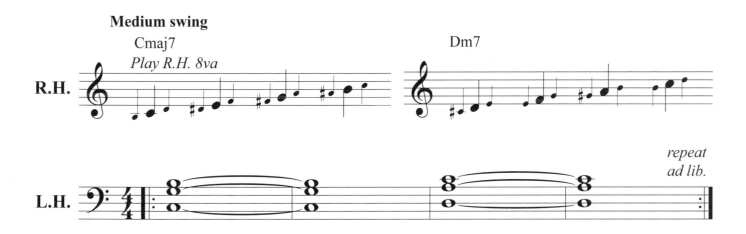

(G is the chord tone)

The L.H. changes chords every two measures.
You can play solo, with your teacher, or with the recording.

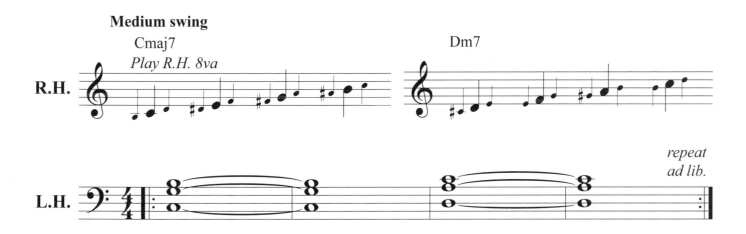

Teacher: If this improv is too difficult, the student can improvise on just the white keys.

Teacher Part: (Student plays as written)

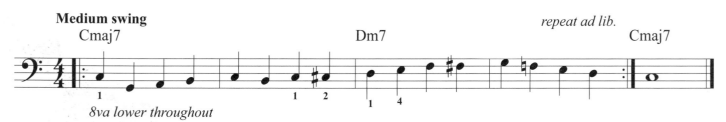

APPENDIX

Two Cycles on ii-V-I

This is a good drill for ii-V-I. Both cycles together contain all the major ii-V-I progressions.

Another way to practice it is by playing only the treble clef, with your L.H.
You can play some of the chords down an octave if they sound too high.

Cycle 1

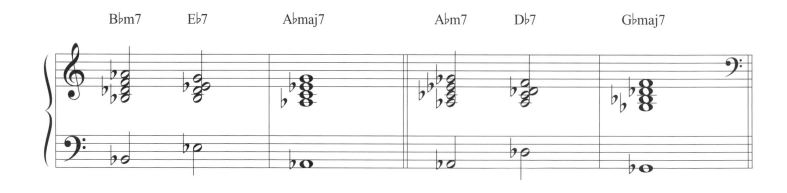

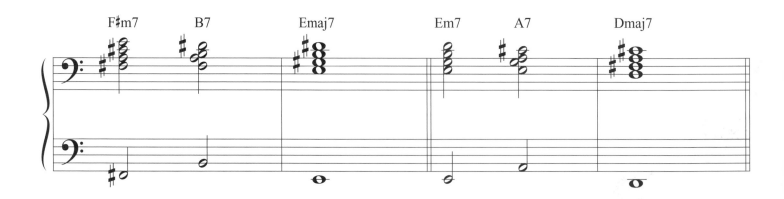

Cycle 2

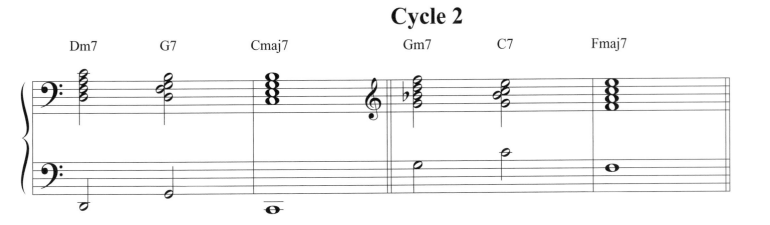

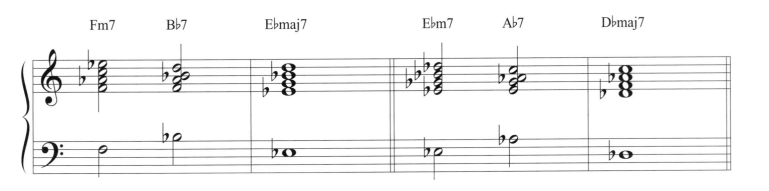

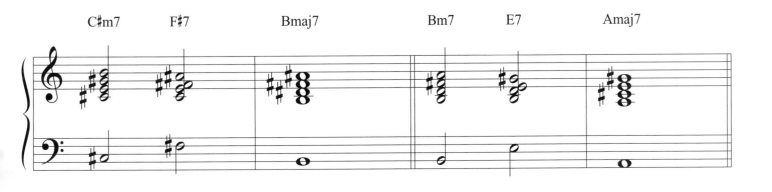

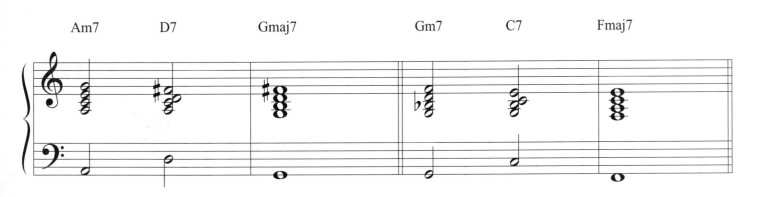

42

Combining Chords with Scales

You've learned four different 7th chords: dominant 7th, major 7th, minor 7th, and half-diminished 7th.
Here are some scale patterns that harmonize with them.

C major scale

C major be-bop scale*

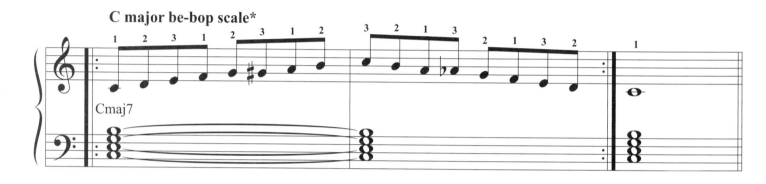

D dorian mode**

Minor be-bop scale***

* The major be-bop scale is a major scale with an extra note between the 6th and 7th scale degrees.

** Dorian mode is built on the 2nd degree of a major scale.
For instance, D dorian uses the notes of the key of C major (D E F G A B C D).
You can also think of it as a natural minor scale with a raised 6th scale degree.

*** The minor be-bop scale is a dorian mode with an extra note between the 3rd and 4th scale degrees.

G mixolydian mode*

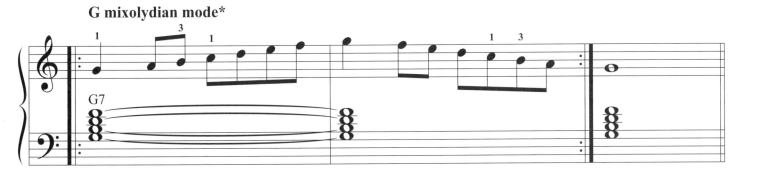

G dominant be-bop scale**

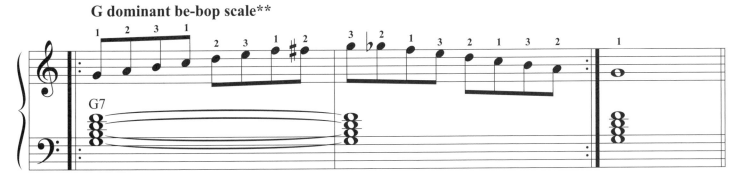

B diminished scale***

Power Blues Scale—Key of C

*The mixolydian mode is built on the 5th degree of a major scale.
  For instance, G mixolydian uses the notes of the key of C major (G A B C D E F G).
  You can also think of it as a major scale with a lowered 7th scale degree.

**The dominant be-bop scale is a mixolydian mode with an extra note between the 7th and 8th scale degrees.

***The diminished scale has an alternating pattern of whole and half steps (W H W H W H W H).

FJH2248

Discography

Below are some classic jazz albums, listed in chronological order, with a recommended song from each album.

Art Tatum, Piano Starts Here (1949, released 2008), Sony, "Tea For Two"
Despite being nearly blind from birth, Tatum revolutionized piano improvisation with technique and improvisation so breathtaking he was sometimes accused of using a second pianist on his recordings.

Charlie Parker, Genius of Charlie Parker (1949-1954, released 2005), Savoy Jazz, "Now's the Time"
"Bird's" early Savoy recordings are a good introduction into this legendary saxophonist's bop style, which has influenced generations of jazz musicians.

Erroll Garner, Concert by the Sea (1955), Columbia, "Autumn Leaves"
Recorded in a converted church in Carmel, California, this classic album demonstrates Garner's rich, orchestral voicings with rhythmic left-hand accompaniments.

Bud Powell, Jazz Giant (1956), Norgran, "Sweet Georgia Brown"
This album was recorded in 1949, and demonstrates why Powell has been called "The Charlie Parker of Piano," with intricate bop licks on tunes like *Sweet Georgia Brown.*

John Coltrane, Blue Train (1957), Blue Note, "Moment's Notice"
An iconic figure in jazz history for his tenor sax playing, Coltrane's improvisatory prowess is on display in this album, which features four original Coltrane tunes, including *Moment's Notice.*

Thelonious Monk/John Coltrane, At Carnegie Hall, Monk & Trane (1957, released 2005), Blue Note, "Epistrophy"
This meeting of two jazz giants features some of Monk's best-known songs, such as *Epistrophy,* in an exciting live performance.

Miles Davis, Kind of Blue (1959), Columbia, "So What"
One of the best-selling jazz albums of all time, *Kind of Blue* demonstrates Miles Davis' evolution from bop to modal jazz. Pianists should pay special attention to the harmonic explorations and voicings of pianist Bill Evans.

Dave Brubeck, Time Out (1959), Columbia, "Take Five"
The Dave Brubeck Quartet, with Brubeck on the piano, explored a variety of time signatures on this album, which blends cool jazz and a West Coast style. *Take Five* is a must for any jazz pianist's playlist.

Bill Evans, Sunday at Village Vanguard (1961), Original Jazz Classics, "Alice in Wonderland"
Classically trained Evans used composers such as Debussy and Ravel as influences on his modal harmonies and chord substitutions. The live recordings of his trio at the Village Vanguard are great examples of dialogue and interplay between the piano and other instruments.

Oscar Peterson, Night Train (1962), Verve, "Night Train"
This album offers a great introduction to the creative variety of Oscar Peterson, one of the most prolific jazz pianists of all time.

Herbie Hancock, Maiden Voyage (1965), Blue Note, "Maiden Voyage"
An innovator of the "post-bop" sound, Hancock incorporated rock influences and synthesizers into his jazz compositions, such as *Maiden Voyage.*

Horace Silver, Song For My Father (1965), Blue Note, "Song for My Father"
Silver integrated a variety of styles into his music, including African and Latin-American musical influences, gospel music, and funk. His album *Song for My Father* was recorded after a trip to Brazil, and shows Silver's interest in the bossa nova style.

McCoy Tyner, The Real McCoy (1967), Blue Note, "Four by Five"
Tyner's work with John Coltrane is clear in this album, which demonstrates a strong blues influence, and an articulated right-hand soloing technique.

Chick Corea, Light As a Feather (1972), Polydor, "Spain"
An innovator in the fusion movement of the 1970s, Corea's album *Light As a Feather* features his most famous composition *Spain,* in which a samba-like theme and improvisatory sections are repeated.

Weather Report, Heavy Weather (1977), Columbia, "Birdland"
An American jazz fusion band in the 1970s, Weather Report explored a variety of instruments and orchestrations. Pianists should pay special attention to the sonic experimentations of keyboardist Joe Zawinul in tunes such as *Birdland.*

Wynton Marsalis, Standard Time, Vol. 1 (1987), CBS/Columbia, "Caravan"
A key figure in jazz education, Marsalis' attention to pay tribute to jazz legends is evident in his version of Duke Ellington's *Caravan.*

Marcus Roberts, Alone With Three Giants (1990), Novus, "Mood Indigo"
Blind since his youth, Roberts received his big break as Wynton Marsalis' pianist. In his subsequent solo recordings, Roberts has often paid tribute to jazz legends, as is evidenced in this recording of Ellington's *Mood Indigo.*

Brad Mehldau, Day is Done (2005), Nonesuch, "She's Leaving Home"
One of the most influential contemporary jazz pianists, Mehldau specializes in his jazz trio work, with his inventive, virtuosic arrangements (often of popular songs like the Beatles' *She's Leaving Home.*)

FJH JAZZ LIBRARY

EARLY ELEMENTARY

In Recital® with Jazz, Blues, & Rags–Book 1   FJH1739
Edited by Helen Marlais

ELEMENTARY

In Recital® with Jazz, Blues, & Rags–Book 2   FJH1740
Edited by Helen Marlais

Performance Jams–Book 1 with CD   FJH1672
Kevin Olson

Pop Improv   FJH2125
Edwin McLean

LATE ELEMENTARY

Color Me Jazz, Book 1   FJH2018
Edited by Lee Evans

In Recital® with Jazz, Blues, & Rags–Book 3   FJH1741
Edited by Helen Marlais

Performance Jams–Book 2 with CD   FJH1673
Kevin Olson

Pop Improv   FJH2125
Edwin McLean

EARLY INTERMEDIATE

Be Cool—Play Jazz!   FJH1359
Kevin Costley

Blues Improv   FJH2248
Edwin McLean and Kevin Olson

Color Me Jazz, Book 2   FJH2115
Edited by Lee Evans

In Recital® with Jazz, Blues, & Rags–Book 4   FJH1742
Edited by Helen Marlais

In the Key of Jazz–Book 1   FJH1738
Kevin Olson and Edwin McLean

Jazz & Blues, Op. 37–Book 1   FJH1403
Robert Schultz

Quiet Waters (solo sheet)   S4104
Carol Matz

INTERMEDIATE

Bayou Boogaloo (solo sheet)   S4012
Edwin McLean

Cool Blue (1 piano/4 hands)   E1041
Carolyn Miller

Cuban Nights (solo sheet)   S4014
Kevin Olson

Gumshoes   FJH1696
Jason Sifford

In Recital® with Jazz, Blues, & Rags–Book 5   FJH1743
Edited by Helen Marlais

In the Key of Jazz, Book 2   FJH2012
Kevin Olson and Edwin McLean

In Tune With Jazz & Blues   FJH1244
Arranged by Carol Matz

Jazz & Blues, Op. 37–Book 2   FJH1404
Robert Schultz

Jazz Improv   FJH2248
Edwin McLean and Kevin Olson

¡Olé!   FJH2038
Lee Evans

LATE INTERMEDIATE

¡Fiesta!   FJH2140
Lee Evans

From Hanon to Jazz   FJH1348
Bert Konowitz

In Recital® with Jazz, Blues, & Rags–Book 6   FJH1744
Edited by Helen Marlais

Jazz & Blues, Op. 37–Book 3   FJH1405
Robert Schultz

Jazzed Up! Christmas   FJH1270
Arranged by Kevin Olson

Jazzed Up! Classics   FJH1351
Arranged by Kevin Olson

Jazzed Up! Folk Songs   FJH1293
Arranged by Kevin Olson

Nightworks   FJH2158
Edwin McLean

out...standing (1 piano/6 hands)   E1062
Kevin Olson

River Rhythms   FJH1582
Kevin Olson

EARLY ADVANCED

**In Recital® for the Advancing Pianist
Jazz & Blues**   FJH2087
Edwin McLean and Kevin Olson /Edited by Helen Marlias

Jazz Nocturnes–Volume One   FJH1190
Edwin McLean

Jazz Nocturnes–Volume Two   FJH1350
Edwin McLean

Jazz Suite (1 piano/4 hands)   E1024
Kevin Olson

ADVANCED

Advanced Jazzed Up! Christmas   FJH2090
Arranged by Kevin Olson

A Smooth Jazz Christmas   FJH1401
Arranged by Roger House

REFERENCE

The FJH Keyboard Chord Encyclopedia   FJH1434
Edwin McLean/Derek Richard